Geometry 3D & 2D
Go Figure!
Grades 1-3
Black & White Version

Geometry
3D & 2D Shapes
(Grades 1-3)

Go Figure! Circle! Match & Tell!

www.butterflybooks.ca

BRAIN Developing:
- Spacial Functioning;
- Memory;
- Cognition
- 3 Games in 1

CIRCLE!

(like Concentration. Any number of Players.)

To Play: All cards are facedown on a table in the shape of a Circle. For each turn, 2 cards are flipped up. The object of the game is to turn over pairs of cards that equal and match. There are 16 sets of 2 cards that match. (A-P). In turn, each player chooses two cards and turns them face up. If they match, the player wins the pair, gains a point and plays again. If they don't match, they are turned face down again and play passes to the player on the left. The game ends when the last card has been picked up.

Wildcards can be used to match any card.

WINNER: One with the Most Matches.

GO FIGURE!
(like Go Fish! . 2-4 Players)

4 cards are dealt to each player. Remaining cards are spread facedown in the shape of a Circle. Each player has a turn asking one of the others for a Card to try and make a match of any figure on one of their cards. There are 16 sets of 2 cards that match (A-P). If player has the card that is equal to a given pair to the asker. If the player doesn't have the card requested, he/she says to the asker "Go Figure!" First player then picks any card from the Big Circle. If a match, the pair is set aside and the player has another turn. If no cards left in the hold, another is chosen from the Circle. If the card doesn't match, the player keeps the new card. Next player does the same.

WINNER: One with the Most Matches.

MATCH & TELL!

To Play: One or more cards are dealt to each player depending on number of players, choosing cards based on sets (A-P). There are 2 in each set, 16 sets. Number of cards to each player has to be even. Example: If 8 players, each has 1 different cards from A-P. OR each has 1 card from A-D. If 16 players, each has 1 card from 1 sets A-G, or H-O.

Each player looks at his or her card. Each player walks the room randomly, looking for another player who has a matching card to theirs. Those 2 players then join together to form a Team, sharing with each other what is on their cards. Once matched up, Each Team, then lines up in the Class in Alphabetical Order A to P, and timed is Show and Tell of their Card Sets, saying aloud the Name of the Shape.

WINNER: Team that has the most fun.

Square (2D)

L

Angle

Blue Butterfly Books™

2

DEDICATION

This Book is dedicated to:

The Karner Blue Butterfly   [1]in All Stages of Life,
And Reilly Hynes, my Handsome Nephew

4

Copyright

Blue Butterfly Books Math & Science Activities are Published by:

Blue Butterfly Books™
Victoria BC
Canada V8S 4H9
www.ButterflyBooks.ca

Copyright ©, Sheila M. Hynes, *Blue Butterfly Books*™
All rights reserved. This book or parts thereof may not be reproduced in any form without permission.   Please visit our website for more information: www.butterflybooks.ca

ISBN-13: 978-0-9920530-4-8
ISBN-10: 0992053048

For other affordable, downloadable and printable Math and Science Games, feel free to visit:
www.math-lessons.ca
www.science-lessons.ca
Printed in the USA

Team Members for this Publication:
Editor: Sheila M. Hynes, *BA Hons, MES, York*
Contributor: Brian Stocker, *BA, MA, Santa Monica*
Contributor: D. A. Stocker, *BA, M Ed, Victoria*
Contributor: Dr. G.A. Stocker, *DDS, Toronto*

Copyright © 2013, by *Blue Butterfly Books*™ , Sheila M. Hynes. ALL RIGHTS RESERVED. No part of this book may be reproduced or transferred in any form or by any means, graphic, electronic, or mechanical, including photocopying, recording, web distribution, taping, or by any information storage retrieval system, without the written permission of the author.

Notice: *Blue Butterfly Books* makes every reasonable effort to obtain from reliable sources accurate, complete, and timely information about the tests covered in this book. Nevertheless, changes can be made in the tests or the administration of the tests at any time and *Blue Butterfly Books* makes no representations or warranties of any kind, expressed or implied, about the completeness, accuracy, reliability, suitability or availability with respect to the information contained in this document for any purpose. Any reliance you place on such information is therefore strictly at your own risk.

The author(s) shall not be liable for any loss incurred as a consequence of the use and application, directly or indirectly, of any information presented in this work. Sold with the understanding, the author is not engaged in rendering professional services or advice. If advice or expert assistance is required, the services of a competent professional should be sought.

The company, product and service names used in this book are for identification purposes only. All trademarks and registered trademarks are the property of their respective owners. *Blue Butterfly Books* is not affiliate with any educational institution.

Table of Contents

Sustainability and Eco-Responsibility

Here at *Blue Butterfly Books*, trees are valuable to Mother Earth and the health and wellbeing of everyone. Minimizing our ecological footprint and effect on the environment, we choose *Create Space*, an eco-responsible printing company.

Electronic routing of our books reduces greenhouse gas emissions, worldwide. When a book order is received, the order is filled at the printing location closest to the client. Using environmentally friendly publishing technology, of the *Espresso* book printing machine, *Blue Butterfly Books* are printed as they are requested, saving thousands of books, and trees over time. This process offers the stable and viable alternative keeping healthy sustainability of our environment. All paper is acid-free, and interior paper stock is made from 30% post-consumer waste recycled material. Safe for children, *Create Space* also verifies the materials used in the print process are all CPSIA-compliant.

By purchasing this *Blue Butterfly Book*, you have supported Full Recovery and Preservation of The Karner Blue Butterfly. Our logo is the Karner Blue, *Lycaeides melissa samuelis*, a rare and beautiful species whose only flower for propogation is the blue lupin. The Karner Butterfly is mostly found in the Great Lakes Region of the U.S.A. Recovery planning is in action, for the return of Karner Blue in Canada led by the National Recovery Strategy. The recovery goals and objectives are aimed at recreating suitable habitats for the butterfly and encourage the growth of blue lupines - the butterfly's natural ideal habitat.

For more info on the Karner Blue Butterfly feel free to visit:

http://www.albanypinebush.org/conservation/wildlife-management/karner-blue-butterfly-recovery

http://www.wiltonpreserve.org/conservation/karner-blue-butterfly.

http://www.natureconservancy.ca/en/what-we-do/resource-centre/featured-species/karner_blue.html.

Customization & White Label Service

Have your logo and school name on the front cover in a special edition produced for you're your school or institution; Visit: www.ButterflyBooks.ca

Or Feel Free to Contact us for details at:
info@ButterflyBooks.ca

Other Books, Study Guides, and Activities

Blue Butterfly Books™   also has:

Study Guides for High School and College Entrance in All Disciplines:
www.ButterflyBooks.ca, and;

Math and Science Activites
For our On-Line Downloadable Games and Free Lesson Plans:
www.math-lessons.ca
www.science-lessons.ca

Let's Begin!

Have Fun Learning 2D & 3D Geometry!

This Set of Math Cards is designed to achieve Learning Standard Requirements for Grade Levels 1-3 Mathematics and Communication. They are to be printed to be "Cut-Out" and made into a 38-Card Playing Deck.

Deck Includes: 1 Deck Cover Card, 3 Instruction Cards, 32 Geometry Playing Cards and 2 Wild Cards. 2 Wildcards can be used for any card during play. HAVE FUN!

4 Learning Games are included:
1. Go Figure! (like *Go Fish!*)
2. Circle! (like *Concentration*)
3. Match & Tell!

Games *Go Figure!, Circle!* And, *Match & Tell* are all basic comprehension games.

Brain Developing:
✓ Spacial Functioning
✓ Memory
✓ Cognition
✓ Coordination

Mathematics Learning Objectives:
✓ Levels 1-3 Mathematics and Communication
✓ Identifying (primarily) Basic 3-dimensional and 2-dimensional Geometric Shapes:
✓ 3D figures - cube, sphere, cone, cylinder, and pyramid
✓ 2D figures - square, rectangle, circle, triangle and right triangle
✓ Ray, Line, vertex, edge and face

Communication:
✓ Listening, observation skills to focus attention
✓ Understanding, identification of information
✓ Communication skills and strategies to interact/work effectively with others
✓ Working collaboratively, and perform tasks
✓ Listening and observation skills and strategies to gain understanding
✓ Analyzing, understanding, synthesizing, and evaluating information
✓ Strategies for focusing attention and interpreting information

Geometry2
The translation of the ancient Greek word Geometry is: *"geo"*- "meaning earth", and *"metron"* - meaning "measurement"). It is a branch of mathematics entailing specifics of shape, size, relative position of figures, and the properties of space. A person who works in the field of geometry is called a *Mathematician*, though is also called a *Geometer*. Geometry concerns lengths, areas, and volumes, with elements in the West beginning around 6th Century BC. By the 3rd century, BC geometry was put into an "axiomatic" form by *Euclid*, a famous Mathematician and Geometer.

Later, the field of astronomy – making maps of the positions of the stars and planets, and describing the understanding between their movements, used the field of geometry extensivly for the following 1,500 years.

In *Euclid's* time there was no clear distinction between physical space and geometrical space. The visual nature of geometry makes it more accessible than other areas of mathematics – as well as spatially, brain developing, a more enjoyable and fun Art.

All Reference Material: Wikipedia.com. See EndNotes.

The Next page describes All 3 Games with Specific Instructions; with rest of the 34 Cards.

Teacher's Resources Pages

The following are Notes for Teachers corresponding to the 3 Instructions Deck Cards:

Circle!
(like *Concentration*; any number of Players)

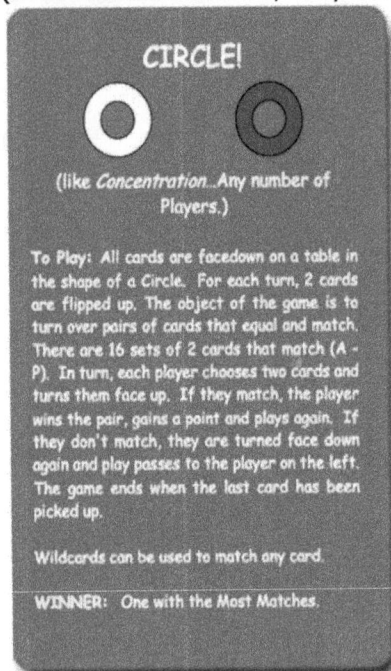

CIRCLE!

(like *Concentration*...Any number of Players.)

To Play: All cards are facedown on a table in the shape of a Circle. For each turn, 2 cards are flipped up. The object of the game is to turn over pairs of cards that equal and match. There are 16 sets of 2 cards that match (A - P). In turn, each player chooses two cards and turns them face up. If they match, the player wins the pair, gains a point and plays again. If they don't match, they are turned face down again and play passes to the player on the left. The game ends when the last card has been picked up.

Wildcards can be used to match any card.

WINNER: One with the Most Matches.

To Play: All cards are facedown on a table in the shape of a Circle. For each turn, 2 cards are flipped up. The object of the game is to turn over pairs of cards that equal and match. There are 16 sets of 2 cards that match (A - P). In turn, each player chooses two cards and turns them face up. If they match, the player wins the pair, gains a point and plays again. If they don't match, the cards are turned face down again and the play passes to the player on the left. The game ends when the last card has been picked up.
Wildcards can be used to match any card.

WINNER: One with the Most Matches.

Go Figure!

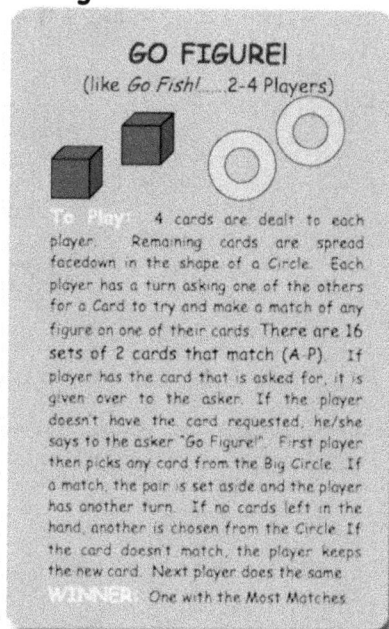

To Play: 4 cards are dealt to each player. Remaining cards are spread facedown in the shape of a Circle. Each player has a turn asking one of the others for a Card to try and make a match of any figure on one of their cards. There are 16 sets of 2 cards that match (A-P). If player has the card that is asked for, it is given over to the asker. If the player doesn't have the card requested, he/she says to the asker "Go Figure!". First player then picks any card from the Big Circle. If a match, the pair is set aside and the player has another turn. If there are no cards left in the hand, another is chosen from the Circle. If the card doesn't match, the player keeps the new card. The Next player does the same.

WINNER: One with the Most Matches.

Match & Tell!

MATCH & TELL!

To Play: One or more cards are dealt to each player depending on number of players, choosing cards based on sets (A-P). There are 2 in each set, 16 sets. Number of cards to each player has to be even. Example: If 8 players, each has 2 different cards from A-P, OR each has 1 card from A-D; if 14 players, each has 1 card from 7 sets A -G, or H-O.

Each player looks at his or her card. Each player walks the room randomly, looking for another player who has a matching card to theirs. Those 2 players then join together to form a Team, sharing with each other what is on their cards. Once matched up, Each Team, then lines up in the Class in Alphabetical Order, A to P, and Gives a Show and Tell of their Card Sets, saying aloud the Name of the Shape.

WINNER: Team that has the most fun.

To Play: One or more cards are dealt to each player depending on the number of players, choosing cards based on sets (A-P). There are 2 in each set, 16 sets. The number of cards to each player has to be even. Example: If there are 8 players, each has 2 different cards from A-P, - or - each has 1 card from A-D; if there are 14 players, each has 1 card from 7 sets A -G, or H-O.

Each player looks at his or her card. Each player walks the room randomly, looking for another player who has a matching card to theirs. Those 2 players then join together to form a Team, sharing with each other what is on their cards. Once matched up, Each Team, then lines up in the Class in Alphabetical Order - A to P - and Gives a Show and Tell of their Card Sets, saying aloud the Name of the Shape.

WINNER: Team that has the most fun.

Geometry
3D & 2D Shapes
(Grades 1-3)
Go Figure! Circle! Match & Tell!

www.butterflybooks.ca

BRAIN Developing:
- ☐ Spacial Functioning;
- ☐ Memory;
- ☐ Cognition
- ☐ 3 Games in 1

CIRCLE!

(like *Concentration*...Any number of Players.)

To Play: All cards are facedown on a table in the shape of a Circle. For each turn, 2 cards are flipped up. The object of the game is to turn over pairs of cards that equal and match. There are 16 sets of 2 cards that match (A - P). In turn, each player chooses two cards and turns them face up. If they match, the player wins the pair, gains a point and plays again. If they don't match, they are turned face down again and play passes to the player on the left. The game ends when the last card has been picked up.

Wildcards can be used to match any card.

WINNER: One with the Most Matches.

GO FIGURE!

(like *Go Fish!*......2-4 Players)

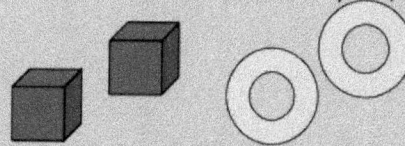

To Play: 4 cards are dealt to each player. Remaining cards are spread facedown in the shape of a Circle. Each player has a turn asking one of the others for a Card to try and make a match of any figure on one of their cards. There are 16 sets of 2 cards that match (A-P). If player has the card that is asked for, it is given over to the asker. If the player doesn't have the card requested, he/she says to the asker "Go Figure!". First player then picks any card from the Big Circle. If a match, the pair is set aside and the player has another turn. If no cards left in the hand, another is chosen from the Circle. If the card doesn't match, the player keeps the new card. Next player does the same.

WINNER: One with the Most Matches.

MATCH & TELL!

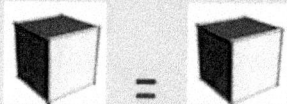

To Play: One or more cards are dealt to each player depending on number of players, choosing cards based on sets (A-P). There are 2 in each set, 16 sets. Number of cards to each player has to be even. Example: If 8 players, each has 2 different cards from A-P, OR each has 1 card from A-D; if 14 players, each has 1 card from 7 sets A -G, or H-O.

Each player looks at his or her card. Each player walks the room randomly, looking for another player who has a matching card to theirs. Those 2 players then join together to form a Team, sharing with each other what is on their cards. Once matched up, Each Team, then lines up in the Class in Alphabetical Order, A to P, and Gives a Show and Tell of their Card Sets, saying aloud the Name of the Shape.

WINNER: Team that has the most fun.

A

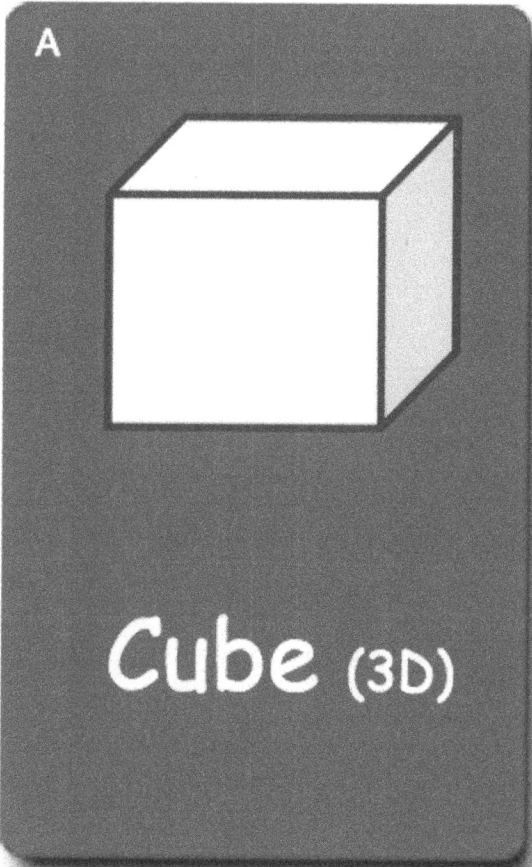

Cube (3D)

A

Cube (3D)

B

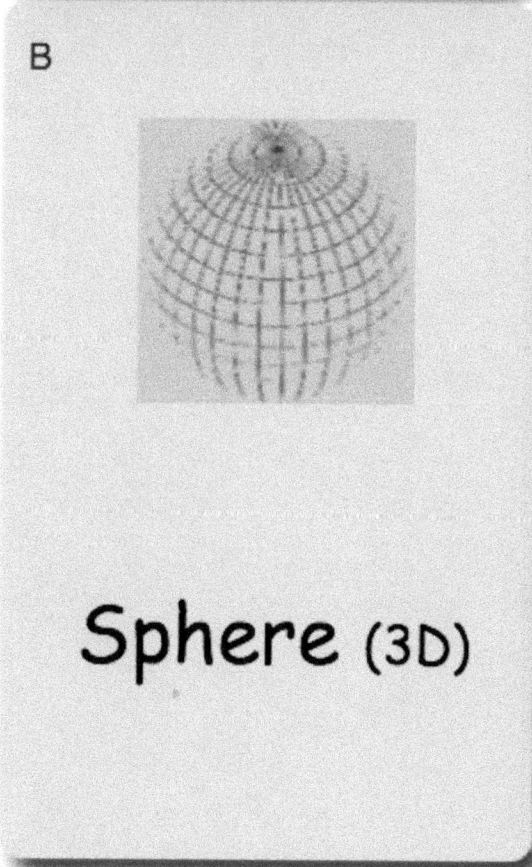

Sphere (3D)

B

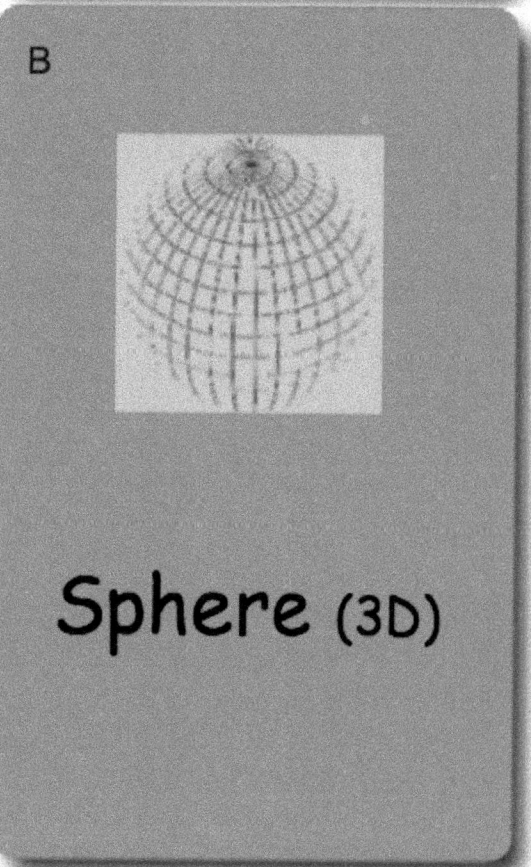

Sphere (3D)

19

C
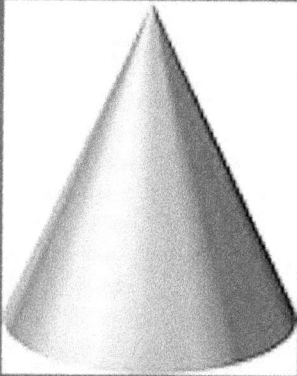
Cone (3D)

C

Cone (3D)

D
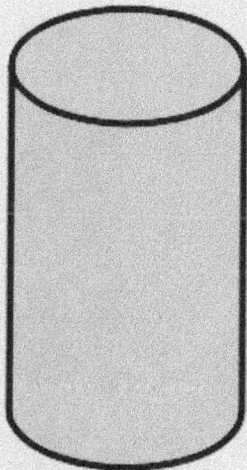
Cylinder (3D)

D
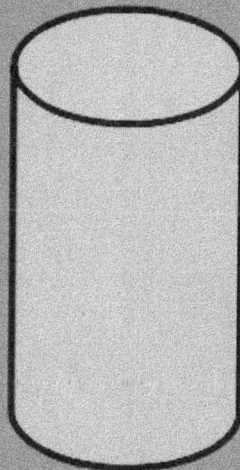
Cylinder (3D)

E

Pyramid (3D)

E

Pyramid (3D)

F

Square (2D)

F

Square (2D)

23

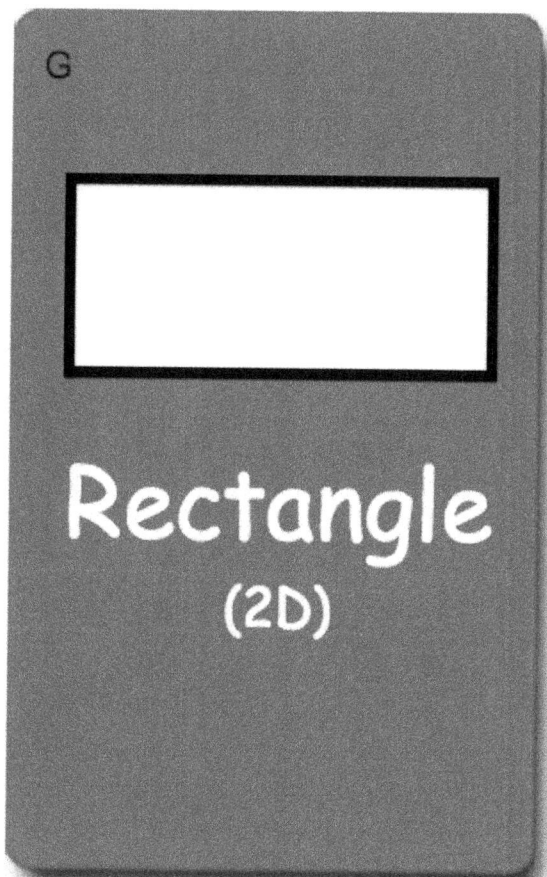

Rectangle
(2D)

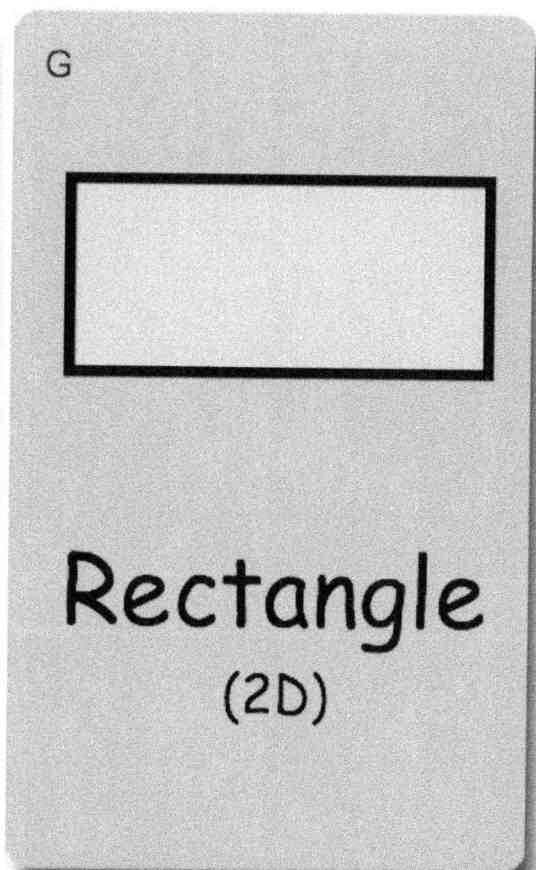

Rectangle
(2D)

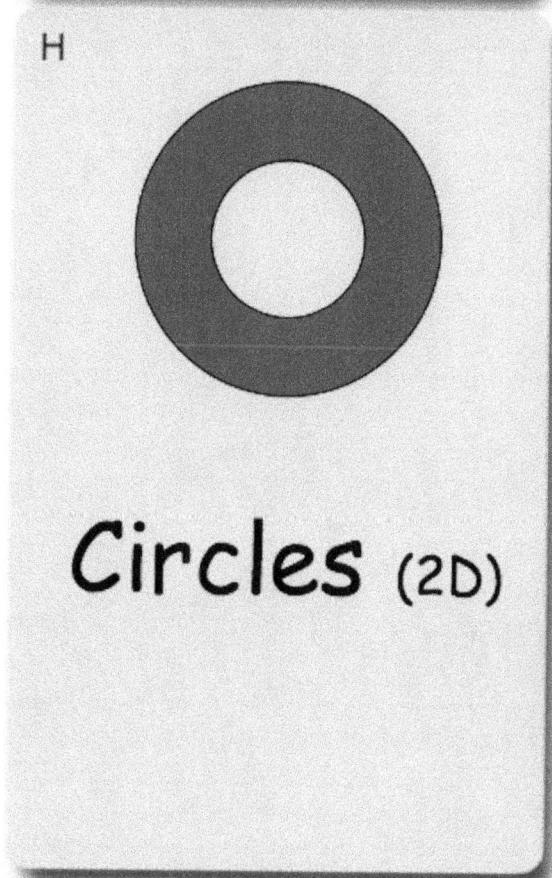

Circles (2D)

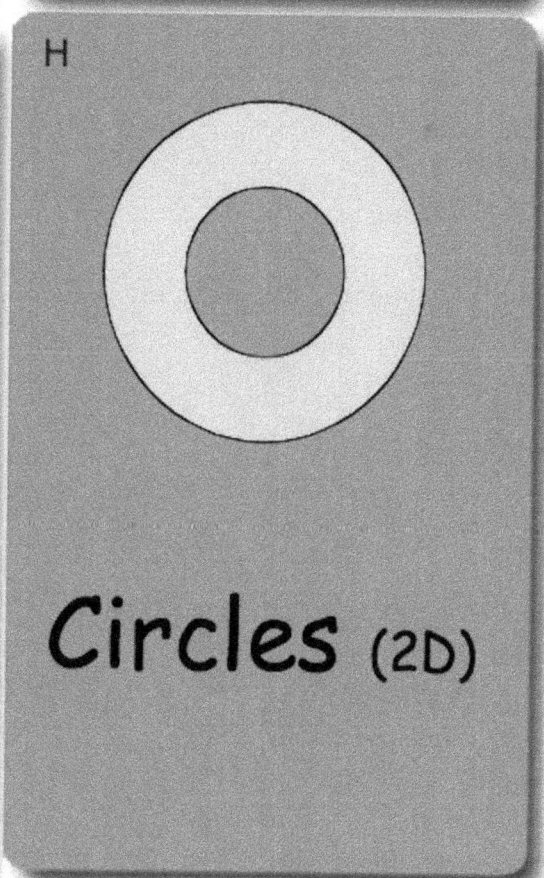

Circles (2D)

I

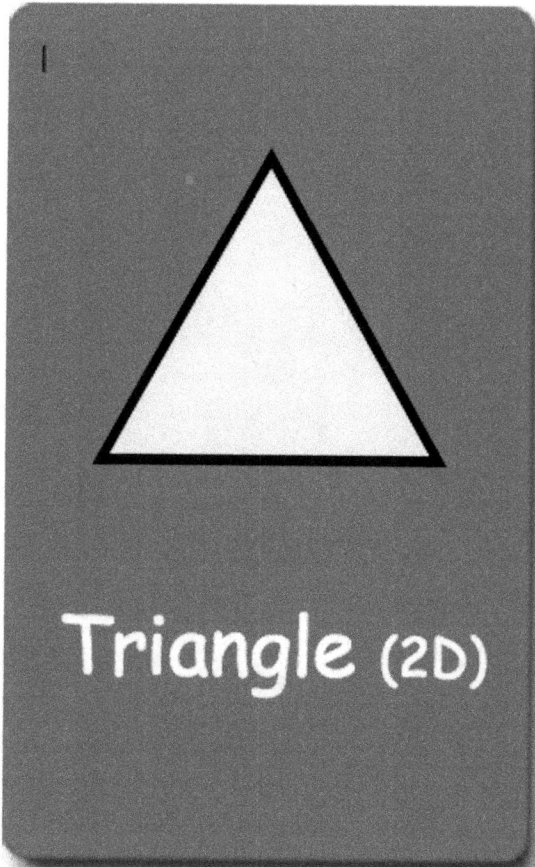

Triangle (2D)

I

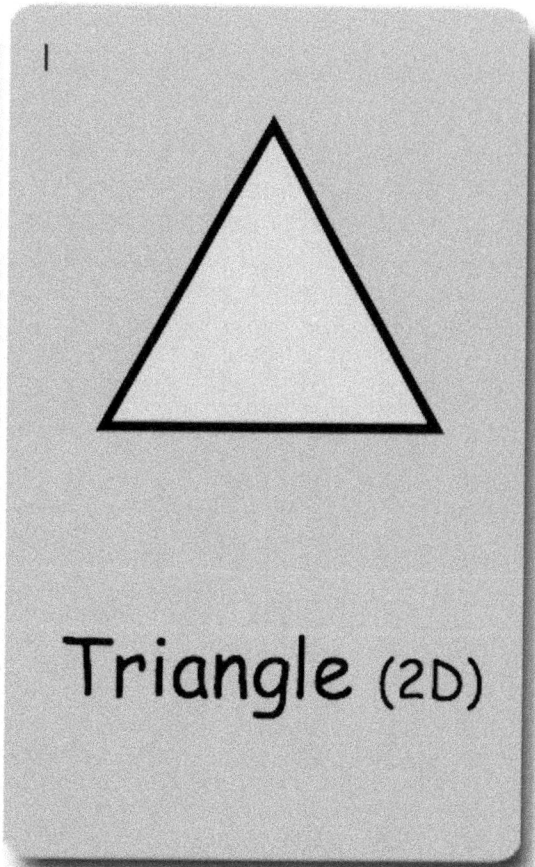

Triangle (2D)

J

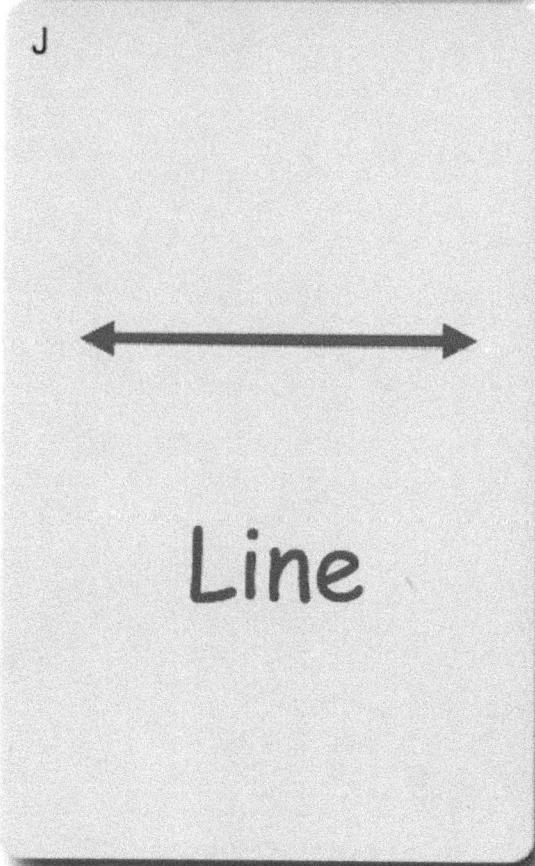

Line

J

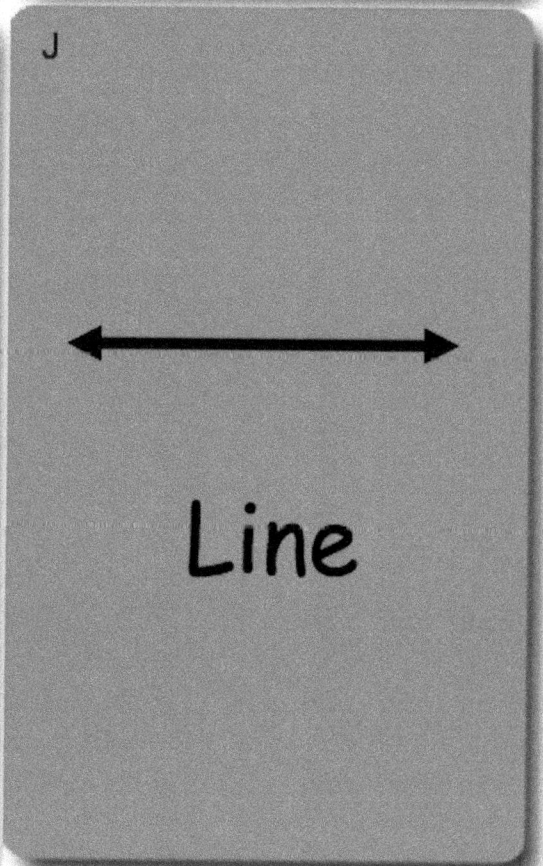

Line

K

Ray

K

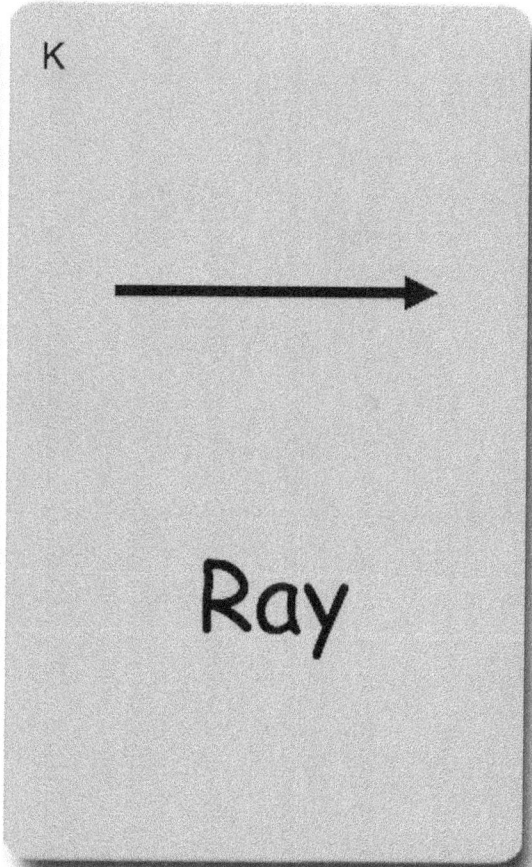

Ray

L

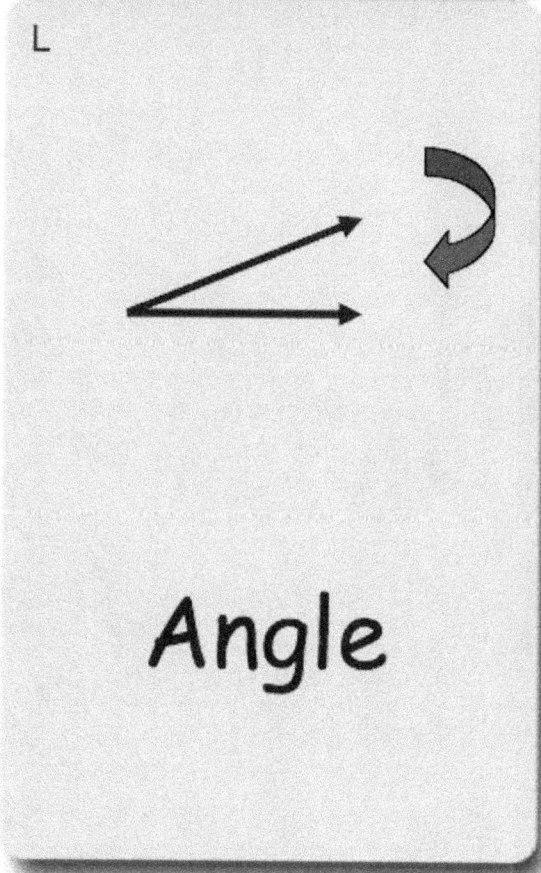

Angle

L

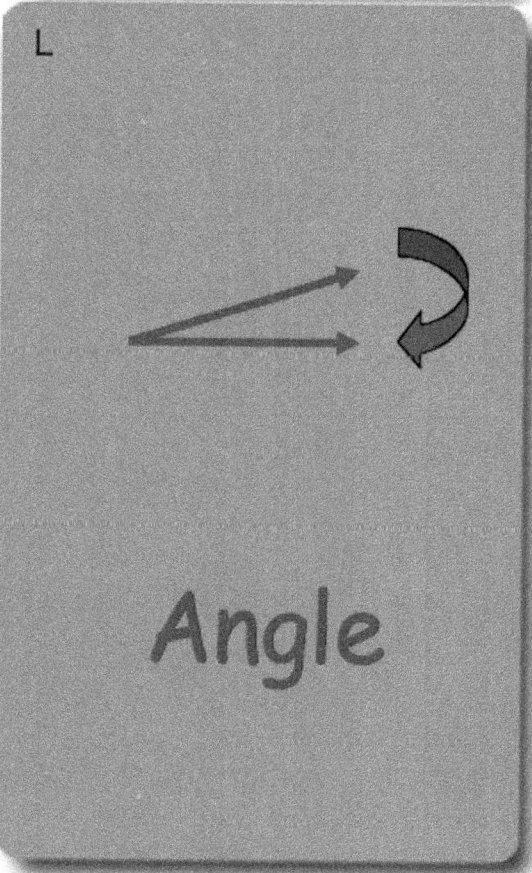

Angle

29

M

3 Vertexes
(3 Corners of a 2D Shape)

M

3 Vertexes
(3 Corners of a 2D Shape)

N

Edges
(Of a 3D Shape)

N

Edges
(Of a 3D Shape)

O

Face
(Of a 3D Shape)

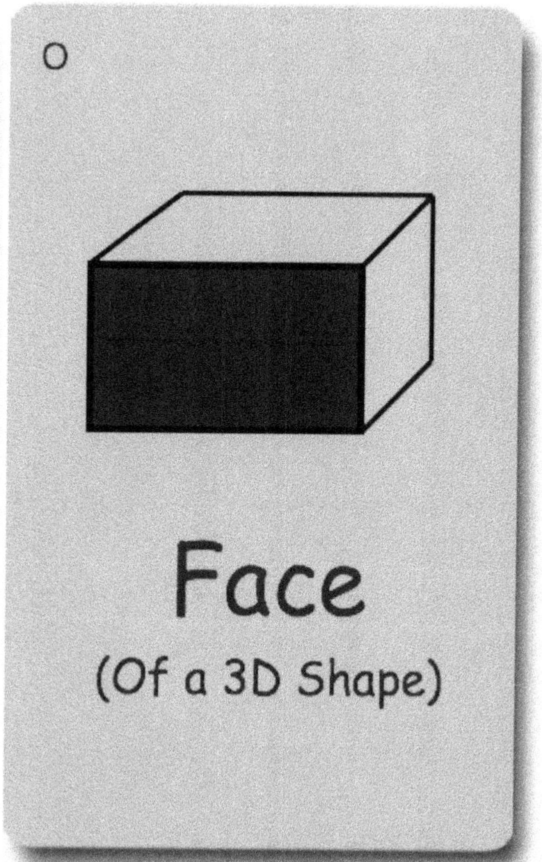

O

Face
(Of a 3D Shape)

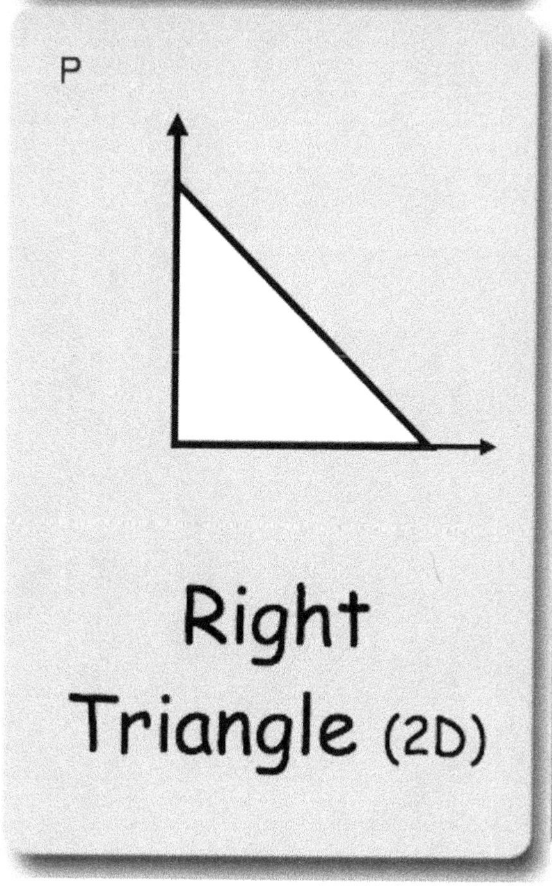

P

Right Triangle (2D)

P

Right Triangle (2D)

WILDCARD

WILDCARD

Blue Butterfly Books ™

www.ButterflyBooks.ca

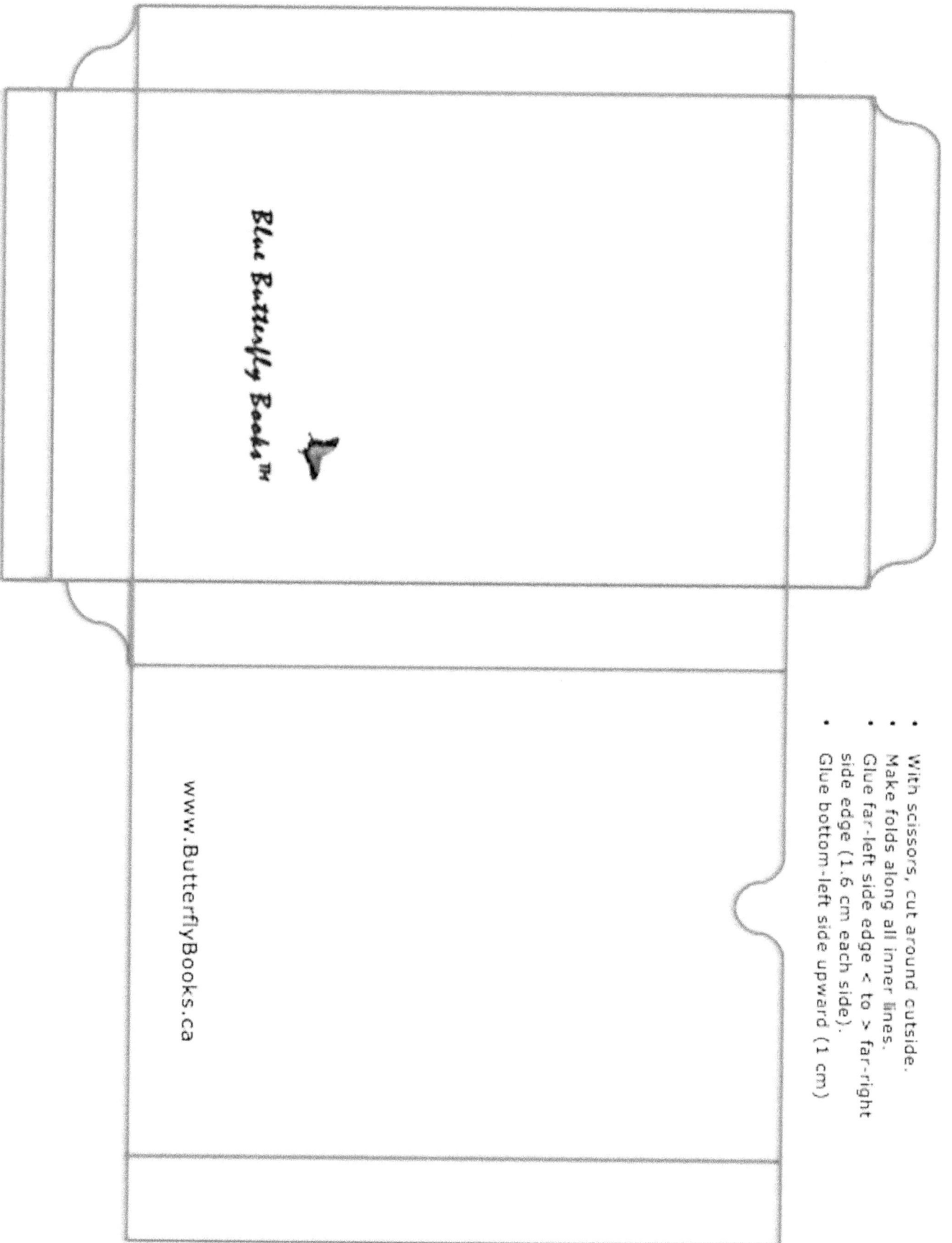

- With scissors, cut around cutside.
- Make folds along all inner lines.
- Glue far-left side edge < to > far-right side edge (1.6 cm each side).
- Glue bottom-left side upward (1 cm)

CONGRATULATIONS!

You made it!! You have made yourself a Deck of Cards that can improve your Learning Geometry in Math for Hours and Hours of Fun. Thank you for playing with

Blue Butterfly Books™ in our mandate to make Learning Math easy and fun!

ENDNOTES:

1. Blue Butterfly. In *Microsoft Clipart*. Retrieved October 15, 2013 from: http://office.microsoft.com/en-CA/images/results.aspx?qu=blue%20butterfly&ex=2#ai:MP900314069|

2. Geometry. In *Wikipedia*. http: //en. wiki/geometry

3. Cube. Uniform polyhedron 222-t012. In *Wikipedia*. Retrieved March 26, 2009 from: http://en. wikipedia.org/wiki/Uniform polyhedron 222-t012

4. Sphere. Sphere wireframe 10deg 6r.svg. In *Wikipedia*. Retrieved March 26, 2009 from: http://en. wikipedia.org/wiki/sphere

5. Cone. In *Wikipedia*. Retrieved March 26, 2009 from: http://en. wikipedia.org/wiki/cone

NOTES